The
Three Tables

Reclaiming an Early Baptist Model
for Deacon Ministry Today

Wyman Lewis Richardson

LEADER'S GUIDE

Table of Contents

A Word of Encouragement to Those Teaching "The Three Tables"

It has been said that the truly great movements in human history come about not as a result of the discovery of new truths but as the result of the rediscovery of old truths. I suspect there is something to that. At the very least the idea should encourage us not to dismiss the past in our feverish addiction to "the next new thing."

At Central Baptist Church in North Little Rock, Arkansas—the church I am honored to pastor—we have lived out the truthfulness of that sentiment in our "rediscovery" of the early Baptist deacon model of The Three Tables. This model is at least as old as the late 1700s and was appealed to by Baptists in both England and America. When these Baptists spoke of The Three Tables, they were speaking of:

1. The Table of the Lord: deacons tending to the Lord's Supper
2. The Table of the Poor: deacons caring for the poor and the needy
3. The Table of the Pastor: in its earliest expressions, the deacons ensuring that the pastor was cared for in a material way

Shortly after I began serving as pastor of Central Baptist we were discussing how to organize ourselves as a deacon body. I mentioned to the body that the earlier Baptist model of The Three Tables might be helpful. After briefly explaining what the tables were a deacon in the room said, "Wait, say that again." Then a fascinating conversation ensued.

I was familiar with The Three Tables and had read and chewed on it a good bit, but, in truth, I was unaware that the issue would even arise in that meeting. I give our deacons all the credit for taking the suggestion and fleshing it out in the wonderful way that they have.

After there was agreement in the room that this model might be of real service to us in our particular situation, we began to discuss what a reclaiming of this model might look like. Our deacons finally landed on an idea. At the end of the meeting we had decided upon creating three rotating teams within our deacon body that correspond to the three tables. Every four months the teams rotate. Thus, every year every deacon will serve each of the tables. As there is no longer a necessity for deacons to serve The Table of the Pastor by raising his salary each month, we have interpreted this table to mean any and every way that the deacon body can be of assistance to me. I value this table greatly, just as I value the other two.

For twelve years now we have stayed with this model. It has become a helpful model, a helpful rediscovery of an old truth. The genius of this model is that it enables us to organize all of the various functions of the deacons into three solidly biblical categories. While the specific terminology of The Three Tables is not *explicitly* in scripture, we are happy to argue along with many of our forebears that this model has been proven to be an effective tool in the organization of the various tasks placed upon deacons in the New Testament. Furthermore, the model of the three tables is flexible enough to be adaptable to the particulars and uniqueness of congregational practice in the modern age yet is defined enough to at least caution churches and deacon bodies against wandering too far afield from practices that should be seen as primary for the deacon body in any church.

There is something to be said for a good model, even if the model is from many years ago. I would like to propose that The Three Tables be brought out of the dusty history books on our shelves and be put "on the table" for consideration.

Teaching the Course

If you are teaching The Three Tables course, know that you are undertaking an exciting and creative journey of what is called *retrieval*. That is, you are going into the past, extracting a forgotten treasure, polishing it off, and asking modern deacons and pastors and churches to ask themselves an important question: "Might this have value for us today?"

The Three Tables is a seven-session deacon training course that asks deacons in Baptist or baptistic churches to consider the creative ways in which they might reclaim the older Baptist idea that deacons are called to serve three tables: The Table of the Lord (the Lord's Supper), The Table of the Poor (benevolence), and The Table of the Pastor (assisting the pastor in various ways). It does this by showing how this model was valued by those who came before us, by showing how this model is consistent with the biblical picture of deacons, and by showing how this model can help deacon bodies in Baptist and baptistic churches today reclaim their vision and mission.

This course has some unique features when compared to other courses. For instance, it includes numerous quotations from Baptist history. These quotations are intended to prove definitively that this approach to organizing deacon bodies was firmly entrenched in earlier Baptist life. It is also intended to demonstrate that what many deacon bodies might consider "the way we have always done it" (i.e., the corporate board model) is actually very clearly undercut by the much earlier model of The Three Tables. There are also some quotations from earlier Christian history. Let me encourage you to have your students read aloud as many of these as possible. Remind them of the great value of these statements: we are getting to hear what our ancestors thought about the important matter of deacons and how they should be organized.

Throughout this leader's guide you will find "Teaching Tips" in the footnotes that will provide either further information on the topic at hand or actual tips for how most effectively to communicate that portion of the study. It will be very important that you prepare thoroughly for each session by reading the material for that session as well as the "Teaching Tips." What is more, the fill-in-the-blank answers are provided as well as proposed answers to many of the discussion questions.

Let me also encourage you to strike the right tone when you teach this course. The material and model that you will be presenting will strike some of your students as unusual. "The Three Tables" model has not been used for many years! You are, in essence, showing the family a wonderful heirloom that will inevitably cause some to ask, "Now what exactly is this?" By the time you are through teaching this course, the family should be saying, "Ah! So that's what that is! What an interesting idea. Perhaps this could help us today!"

Furthermore, this model should not be presented in a narrow or restrictive way. Baptist churches have more diversity in how we are organized today than we have had at any other time in our past. The point of this course is not to say, "You must clear the deck and do only this!" Rather, it is to say, "In what ways might this model of The Three Tables work with your church and its structures and systems?" It is not, in other words, an all-or-nothing proposition. Some churches may wish to have their deacon bodies embrace all three tables. For other churches it may be one or two of the tables. Remember that some churches have, for instance, separate benevolence or Lord's Supper teams that may or may not involve deacons. This course is not asking that those teams be done away with. It does dare to ask whether or not, even in these cases, deacons might have some part in these ministries.

The Three Tables model should be seen as a creative prompt and not as a rigid template. As I argue in the material, there is validity to this earlier model, and yet scripture does leave some measure of latitude concerning the details of how we organize ourselves.

That being said, the model of The Three Tables is an interesting, biblically-informed, viable model that could truly help churches today. Even granting the qualifications just mentioned, this material should be presented enthusiastically and with a sense of great promise, for promising it is! I can speak personally to how this model has brought a sense of clarity to the church I pastor. I can also speak to how intrigued by this model those pastors and deacons that I have been privileged either to speak to about this model or teach in a formal setting have been by it.

Throughout the workbook you and your students will encounter the following three signs:

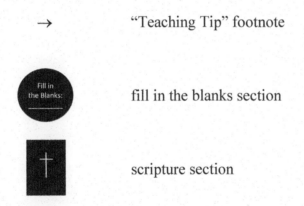

$\rightarrow$ "Teaching Tip" footnote

Fill in the Blanks: fill in the blanks section

         scripture section

It is hoped that this study will lead you and your deacons to engage scripture, the history of the Baptist family, and the history of the wider church in a thoughtful and constructive manner resulting in healthy, effective deacon bodies and strengthened churches.

Deacon bodies and pastors and churches are hungry to have deacons be the faithful servants that they are depicted as in the New Testament. The Three Tables can be a very helpful tool toward making that biblical vision a reality today.

For Teaching Videos and More Information, Visit
www.thethreetables.com

Session 1
What's at Stake?

Let every preacher, every deacon, and every private member of the church examine himself strictly, as in the presence of the living God, and if he finds that he has been remiss, or negligent in any Christian duty, let him repent, return, and do his first works; let every church be stirred up to use all diligence in all the duties of her charge. In short, a reformation must first begin among professors [i.e., Christians], before we can expect to see it among the unconverted.→

John Jenkins, 18th/19th c. Virginia Baptist pastor[1]

The remark has become common that the office of deacon in our day has become almost *a practical nullity*. This is but too true and should be remedied.

Associational Circular Letter, Brenham, TX, July 11–13, 1862[2]

I. Setting the Stage

In his book *Pastor and Deacons: Servants Working Together*, Ken Howerton wrote:

The deacon's reputation becomes the reputation of the church.[3]

Do you agree with Howerton's statement? Why or why not?→

→ **TEACHING TIP:** Throughout this study, consider having your students read aloud the various statements and quotes that are provided. This gives the students a part in the teaching of the material. Explain that the reason why there are so many quotations from Baptist history in this study is because we are trying to demonstrate (a) that there never was a "golden era" of history in which there were not problems, (b) earlier Baptists dealt with the same issues we deal with today, and, therefore, (c) the voice of those who came before us should be heeded.

→ **TEACHING TIP:** Much is at stake when it comes to whether or not deacons are faithful in the execution of their duties. God notices. The church that deacons are called to serve notices. The deacon's family notices. Indeed, the watching world notices.

II. The Scandal of the Compromised Deacon

Take a moment and read this unflattering depiction of deacons from the late-nineteenth/early-twentieth century.→

> Old Deacon Gray was as mean a man
> As I've seen for many a day;
> He'd steal and lie for the sake of a dime,
> And rob all who came in his way[4]

Poems like this led one pastor in 1906 to observe:

> The newspapers find the name deacon a convenient one when they want to contrast **profession** with **performance**..."

Why is this "contrast" such a tragedy?

> **Because integrity, the witness of the church, and the evangelistic effectiveness of the church hinges upon there being no contrast between our profession and our performance.**

In 1 Timothy 3, Paul stresses with intensity the significance of the character of the deacon.

> [8] Deacons likewise must be dignified, not double-tongued, not addicted to much wine, not greedy for dishonest gain. [9] They must hold the mystery of the faith with a clear conscience. [10] And let them also be tested first; then let them serve as deacons if they prove themselves blameless. [11] Their wives likewise must be dignified, not slanderers, but sober-minded, faithful in all things. [12] Let deacons each be the husband of one wife, managing their children and their own households well. [13] For those who serve well as deacons gain a good standing for themselves and also great confidence in the faith that is in Christ Jesus.

For Paul and for the early church, no contrast between a deacon's *profession* to be a follower of Jesus and servant of the church and his actual *performance* of these professions was permissible. The thought of little poems mocking deacons would have been anathema to Paul!

→ **TEACHING TIP:** This poem and others like it are from an article by Patricia Marks entitled "Holy and Unholy Deacons in Late Nineteenth-Century Popular Verse." You can also mention these other examples from the article: "I've noticed that deacons and deep divines / And pillars of churches, too, / Walk around with a smile when at Coney Isle / And God knows the things they do." And, "An honest man was Deacon Ray / And, though a Christian good / He had one fault,— the love of drink; / For drink he often would. / On almost every Sunday, too, / He would at dinner-time / Indulge to quite a great extent / In good Madeira wine." And one more: And so 'twas not singular that / This good deacon, solemn and fat, / Found a dollar or more. / When collection was o'er / Sticking up in the crown of his hat.

What would you like to be said of you as a deacon years from now? Take the poem above about "Old Deacon Gray," add your name after the words "Old Deacon," and rewrite the rest of it the way you would like for it to be written one hundred years from now about you.

Old Deacon _____

_____

_____

_____

III. The Urgent Need for Resolution→

Read this statement from the 1845 West Union Association of the Kentucky Baptists.

> "*Whereas,* much difficulty has heretofore risen in consequence of the common practice, now in use, in ordaining ministers and deacons; therefore,
>
> "*Resolved,* That we advise the churches to take into consideration the propriety of sending, each year, to the Association, before calling them forth in ordination, such persons as they may desire to call forth to the said offices, and also, of authorizing the Association to appoint a committee to examine into their qualifications and capacity, and if found capable and worthy, to give the applicant a certificate of qualification."[5]

 These Baptists believed that the process of ordaining ministers and deacons in their day had given rise to **much difficulty**.

 Consequently, the West Union Association proposed that the Association conduct a process of **qualification** before the churches proceeded to **ordination**.

→ **TEACHING TIP:** Consider the following as a transition statement: Yes, a deacon body that is not functioning as it ought to function is a scandal. For this reason, historically, Baptists have recognized the need to have well-trained, efficient, biblically-defined, church-edifying, and God-glorifying deacons, even as we have struggled to maintain such. Time and time again the historical record shows moments of concern, exasperation, and proposed solutions that reveal the high view of deacons that Baptists have traditionally held. Sometimes this exasperation caused groups of Baptists to take rather surprising steps. I marvel, for instance, at the actions of the 1845 West Union Association of the Kentucky Baptists who had "such a degree of annoyance" at unsound pastors and deacons that they proposed the following… [Have a student read the statement.]

This is very surprising given the Baptist emphasis on the **autonomy** of the local church.→

 Even so, it does demonstrate how critically important it is that deacon bodies have **integrity**.

 Reminder: "The deacon's reputation becomes the reputation of **the church**."

IV. What We Stand to Gain

Read Paul's words below from 1 Timothy 3.

 [13] For those who serve well as deacons gain a good standing for themselves and also great confidence in the faith that is in Christ Jesus.→

What two things do deacons who serve well "gain":

1. a good standing for themselves
2. great confidence in the faith that is in Christ Jesus

What does this mean?

Faithful deacons gain a good standing in both the church and the world. They are strengthened in their faith as they live out the example of Jesus through lives of service and care for others.

→ **TEACHING TIP:** Anyone who knows anything about how cherished the principle of "local church autonomy" is among Baptists will share my surprise at this. Baptists are quite averse to having outside bodies—even bodies, like associations, with which they voluntarily associate and which they financially support—interfere in the inner workings of local congregational life. This principle of church autonomy is reflected in the resolution's language of "advising" the churches to "take into consideration" the proposal and of the churches "authorizing the Association" to execute the resolution. Even so, it is fascinating that the association would feel the need to ask the churches to allow it to take a paternal role over the congregations in the choosing of pastors and deacons. Specifically, among the Kentucky Baptists of this region and time, they proposed that the names of candidates for pastoral and deacon ministry be submitted first to the Association for examination! I have no idea whether or not this proposal was honored, but it shows how seriously these Baptists took the perceived degradation of the office of pastor and/or deacon.

→ **TEACHING TIP:** Philip Towner has offered the interesting observation that the phrase "good standing" actually may hint at the reformation of the office of deacon in first century Ephesus (the church that Timothy served). He writes: "The apostasy of some . . . deacons in Ephesus almost certainly lowered opinions about leaders and leadership in the church and in the minds of outsiders. So confidence in the office and in the people filling that office needed to be restored."

What does "a good standing for themselves and also great confidence in the faith that is in Christ Jesus" look like? Read the statement below about Thomas Jones, a Virginia Baptist deacon of the 18th century, which was written after his death.

> Mr. Thomas Jones…was also a deacon of this church, and may be said to rank in the first grade. From the day he professed godliness until his death he appears to have devoted his whole soul to his Master's service. It is not likely that any private character ever did more good in so short a time. Though in affluent circumstances, he knew how to use this world as not abusing it. After a lingering illness he also fell asleep anno 1805.[6]

For what was Thomas Jones remembered?

His godliness. His devotion to the cause of Christ. His good deeds. He handling of money rightly and with integrity.

V. A Challenge and a Decision

Read the statement below from Matt Smethurst concerning a fascinating historical example of a body of believers rallying to protect deacons.

> The Nazis . . . did not like deacons.
>
> After the Netherlands fell to Germany in 1940, deacons in the Dutch Reformed Church rose up to care for the politically oppressed, supplying food and providing secret refuge. Realizing what was happening, the Germans decreed that the office of deacon should be eliminated. Responding in a General Synod on July 17, 1941, the Dutch believers resolved, 'Whoever touches the diaconate interferes with what Christ has ordained as the task of the church.'…Whoever lays hand on *diakonia* lays hands on worship!'"
>
> The Germans backed down.[7]

The Dutch believers argued that whoever hinders deacons "hinders what **Christ** has ordained as the task of the church." If Christ is not pleased with the unbelieving world hindering the work of deacons through persecution, what must He think of *the church* hindering the work of deacons through **neglect**?

Session 2
The Three Tables

The ministers and other brethren, who compose the Georgia Association, to their constituent Christian friends, send greeting:

> Beloved in the Lord—Being again assembled, and somewhat filled with each other's company, and the intelligence received from you; it has seemed good to us, at this time, to address to you a few admonitory remarks on *the official* duty of a Deacon…
>
> We shall take up this subject as it is stated in our last minutes, to wit: "Is it to serve tables, or to attend to the temporal necessities of the Church: [the Lord's Supper], the Poor and the Minister."

The Circular Letter of Rev. Mr. Rhodes to the Baptists of Georgia, 1808[8]

I. Your Model Drives Your Ministry

Thesis: Our **language** defines our **model** and our model drives our **ministry**.→

Deacons were not referred to as "boards" popularly in Baptist churches seemingly until the middle of the 19th century when a Baptist writer named R.B.C. Howell proposed the idea. James Leo Garrett Jr. writes of Howell's proposal:

> R.B.C. Howell in *The Deaconship* (1846) declared that deacons "are not ministers who preach . . . nor mere distributors of alms . . . but serve in a different capacity. They are a board of directors, and have charge of all the secular affairs in the kingdom of Christ."[9]

→ **TEACHING TIP:** Let us be clear: the model that a deacon body adopts will in large measure drive that body's ministry. Every deacon body has a model and the truth of the model can be ascertained not merely through an evaluation of that body's behavior but also through a consideration of that body's language and terminology.

The language of "board" is **corporate**. The language of "body" is **New Testament** (Romans 12:5; 1 Corinthians 12:12-31; Ephesians 4:12, 5:23; Colossians 1:24).→

 We tend to **perform** up or down to the language we employ to define our model.

II. The Three Tables

Many earlier Baptists spoke of the responsibilities of deacons in terms of three tables:

- The Table of the **Lord**
- The Table of the **Poor**
- The Table of the **Pastor**

III. The Three Tables in Baptist History

Consider, for instance, the following account of the ordination of deacons among the Philadelphia Baptists from December 10, 1763.

> The Church met this day, by way of preparation for celebrating the Lord's Supper on the morrow; and to ordain deacons. The Meeting began with prayer from the desk suitable to both designs of the Meeting. Then was delivered a dissertation on the office of a deacon, his qualifications and duty and the manner of his election and instalment in the office. Then the deacons elect, viz. Joseph Moulder, Joseph Watkins and Samuel Miles were brought to the administrator; who laid his hands on each, and prayed in the following words: In the name of the Lord Jesus, and according to the practice of His Apostles towards persons chosen to the deaconship, I lay hands on you, my brother, whereby you are constituted, or ordained a deacon of this church; installed in the office and appointed and

---

→ **TEACHING TIP:** Make clear that this is not to suggest that a deacon body is *sinning* against God if it refers to itself as a "board" or that a deacon body cannot live out a New Testament vision if it refers to itself as a "board." That is not the position of this study. But it is to suggest that insofar as the language of "board" represents corporate America and all that goes along with it, the very terminology may suggest, subtly or otherwise, concepts and assumptions that can, at times, be inimical to a biblical view of the church. In other words, at certain points a deacon body will have to fight against the full implications of the terminology of "board" where that language tempts the deacon body to this or that kind of behavior or mindset that might be inconsistent with the picture of deacons we find in scripture. What we want, then, is a model defined by language *that fits as harmoniously as possible with the New Testament depiction of our ministry.* This is yet another way that the idea of "The Three Tables" is helpful. It employs a biblical picture (table service, Acts 6:2–3) that fits more naturally with deacon ministry than corporate terminology can hope to do. What is more, the *trajectory* of "table" language leads us deeper into the very concept of service whereas as the power and management trajectory of "board" can tempt us to ideas that are not germane to a New Testament picture of deacon service.

empowered to collect and receive her revenues, and to dispose thereof in providing for and serving the Lord's table; and in providing for the table of the Minister and the poor; and in transacting other temporal affairs of the church, that the Minister may not be deterred from the word and prayer, nor the concerns of the family of faith neglected.[10]

Note the general responsibilities of deacons as outlined by the Baptists of Philadelphia:

- The Table of the **Lord**: "providing for and serving the Lord's Table"
- The Table of the **Poor**: "providing for the table of...the poor"
- The Table of the **Pastor**: "providing for the table of the Minister"

Consider also the following insertion into the minutes of the First Baptist Church of Boston from June 18, 1788.

At this period the standing committee of the Pew Proprietors relieved the deacons of most of the financial burden which had rested on them in the older times. The deacons no longer provided for the salary of the minister and the support of public worship. They cared for the poor, attended to discipline, looked after arrangements for the Lord's Supper, and were the pastor's counselors in spiritual matters.[11]→

III. A Model to be Valued

The genius of this model is that it enables us to organize the various functions of the deacon into **three** solidly biblical categories.

Furthermore, the model of the three tables is **flexible** yet establishes **parameters**.→

→ **TEACHING TIP:** Here are some more historical examples you can share if you feel led and time permits. We further see that the Kehukee Baptist Association of North Carolina used the terminology of the three tables in its clearest form. With reference to deacons, the associations of 1788 declared that "their work is to serve tables, that is, the table of the Lord; the table of the minister, and the table of the poor; and for to see that the church makes provision for them," and in 1800 that "deacons ought to be regularly ordained before they use the office of a deacon in any respect." Time and again, the Baptists of yesteryear commended this idea of the three tables. James Pendleton, in his 1878 *Christian Doctrines: A Compendium of Theology*, writes, "As deacons were first appointed 'to serve tables,' it may be well to say that there are three tables for them to serve: 1. The table of the poor; 2. The table of the Lord; 3. The table of the pastor." Nor was this a distinctly American Baptist idea. James Leo Garrett Jr. informs us that the 1773 Charleston Baptist *Summary of Church Discipline* "favorably quoted from the exposition of John Gill of London concerning three tables for which deacons are responsible: the table of the Lord (Lord's Supper); the minister's table (ministerial support), and the table of the poor."

→ **TEACHING TIP:** The genius of this model is that it enables us to organize the various functions of the deacon into three solidly biblical categories. Furthermore, the model of the three tables is flexible enough to be adaptable to the particulars and idiosyncrasies of individual congregational practice yet defined enough to at least caution churches and deacon bodies about wandering too far afield from practices that should be seen as primary for the deacon body in any church. Thus, "The Table of the Lord" may encompass many things: moving the communion table into place for the observance of the Lord's Supper, the purchase of the bread and juice, the cleaning of the trays or instruments of serving the elements, and the practicalities of helping with the dissemination of the elements to the congregation. It might include all of those or it might include only some. It might include elements that have not been mentioned here. Yet the table defined as it is does call the Baptist deacon not to neglect his part in serving the table of the Lord.

Similarly, "The Table of the Pastor" can mean many things. It might refer to the spiritual advice that deacons give to their pastor. It might refer to helping him with visitation in the church. It might, given a specific congregation and their agreed-up organization, mean many things. But the fact that it is called "The *Table* of the Pastor" certainly curtails certain abuses in either direction. The deacon must remember that it is not called "The Guillotine of the Pastor" or the "The Prison of the Pastor." The pastor must remember that it is not called "The Bully Pulpit of the Pastor" or "The Mirror of the Pastor" or "The Platform of the Pastor." No, it is a "table," a place around which people of good will gather for mutual edification in the name of the risen Lord.

Session 3
The First Table: The Table of the Lord

→ But we, after we have thus washed [baptized] him who has been convinced and has assented to our teaching, bring him to the place where those who are called brethren are assembled, in order that we may offer hearty prayers in common for ourselves and for the baptized [illuminated] person, and for all others in every place, that we may be counted worthy, now that we have learned the truth, by our works also to be found good citizens and keepers of the commandments, so that we may be saved with an everlasting salvation. Having ended the prayers, we salute one another with a kiss. There is then brought, to the president of the brethren, bread and a cup of wine mixed with water; and he taking them, gives praise and glory to the Father of the universe, through the name of the Son and of the Holy Ghost, and offers thanks at considerable length for our being counted worthy to receive these things at His hands. And when he has concluded the prayers and thanksgivings, all the people present express their assent by saying Amen. This word Amen answers in the Hebrew language to *genoito* [so be it]. And when the president has given thanks, and all the people have expressed their assent, those who are called by us deacons give to each of those present to partake of the bread and wine mixed with water over which the thanksgiving was pronounced, and to those who are absent they carry away a portion.

Justin Martyr's *First Apology*, chapter LXV (mid-2nd century AD)
[One of the earliest descriptions of a worship service in all of Christian history.]

I. Baptist Continuity with Ancient Christian Worship

Fill in the Blanks:

Baptists have long argued that the basic elements of our worship stand in **harmony** and **continuity** with the basic elements of the worship of the early church.

→ **Teaching Tip:** A good transition at this point might be, "We have been considering Baptist history over the last few hundred years. Now let us go back even further, to the earliest days of Christian history, to one of the earliest descriptions of what we would call a 'worship service' in all of Christian history! Would somebody like to read this statement by Justin Martyr aloud while the rest of us listen carefully?"

As with early Christian history, so too with Baptist history, we find deacons serving The Table of the Lord. Consider the following from the 1834 "Treatise on the Faith of the Freewill Baptists":

> A deacon is a regular or stated servant of the church. As the bishops were appointed to take the charge of souls, it is inferred that the seven appointed to minister to the saints (Acts 6:1–6) were deacons; and that as the former have the oversight of the spiritual concerns of the church, the latter have the charge of its temporal affairs, particularly in serving the tables of the needy. (Acts 6:1–4.) *Though there is no scriptural evidence that serving the Lord's table at communion was required of deacons, it appears that by common consent they have long performed this service in several denominations.*[12]

What we have in the belief held among many Baptists that the deacons should serve the Lord's Supper is an appeal to tradition. →

Robert Fleming, a nineteenth-century Georgia Baptist, in an April 1842 sermon he preached at the deacon ordination service for W.H. Daniel and Talbot X. Reese, acknowledged that while we do not find in scripture an explicit command that deacons alone oversee the table of the Lord, the idea is at least in harmony with the initial service of deacons in Acts 6.

> According to the custom of the churches in our day, the deacons are to serve the Lord's table. This custom, if supported at all from the New Testament, is supported by remote inference. 'It is not reason that we should leave the word of God and serve tables.'…[I]t is inferred that [deacons] should attend to that service which is necessary in order to an observance of the Lord's Supper. The furnishing of the bread and wine…may…be more properly considered as being the duty of the deacons."

II. A Healthy Baptist Posture toward the Question

We agree that scripture does not offer any kind of unambiguous teaching that deacons and deacons *alone* serve the elements. We do say that deacon service at the Lord's table has deep historical attestation, is not in violation of scripture, and seems to work well with the traditional structure of Baptist congregational life as having two offices: that of pastor and that of deacon.

→ **TEACHING TIP:** At this point it should be observed that tradition, rightly understood, can be a good thing, especially in areas of practice, governance, and polity in which the Bible is silent, though it must never become the *main* thing or be elevated to the level of or above scripture. We are not told in the Bible that the deacons distributed the elements of the Lord's Supper *per se*, but then we are not told who distributed them at all! The responsibilities of deacons are not exhaustively spelled out. This means on the one hand that we should not be overly dogmatic and say that *only* deacons can distribute the elements. On the other hand, it is a practice, as we have seen, that is grounded firmly in the early practice of the church, has practical import, and violates no tenet of scripture whatsoever.

Deacon service at The Table of the Lord also harmonizes well with the other tables. Consider the connection between The Table of the Lord and the Table of the Pastor (i.e., in this case, helping the pastor care for the families of the church).

The deacon who distributes the elements will not be seen as a mere **bystander** by the recipients. His physical presence at the table coincides with his **consistent** presence in the lives of those he serves. For this reason, the recipient of the Supper not only will *not* see the servants of the table as mere conveyors of elements, he or she will see the deacon as one who has a hand in calling him or her consistently to the foot of the **cross** therein memorialized.→

Furthermore, the deacons of Central Baptist Church in North Little Rock, AR, link The Table of the Lord and The Table of the Poor together at each observance of the Lord's Supper by collecting a benevolence offering at the doors of the sanctuary as people depart. This offering is an extra offering, in addition to the normal offering, and is administered solely by the deacons.

It is stressed to the congregation that the connection between the Lord's Supper and caring for the poor is organic and **natural**: we give to the poor specifically on these occasions when we memorialize, through the Supper, that Christ gave **all** for us.

III. How Deacons Serve the Table of the Lord→

The ways in which deacon bodies can serve the Table of the Lord include but certainly are not limited to:

- overseeing, maintaining, and purchasing or arranging for the purchase of the elements and other Lord's Supper supplies;

- ensuring that the furniture and instruments of the Supper (the table and plates if such are used) are presentable and in good condition;

→ **TEACHING TIP:** The wisest approach might be that of Baptist scholar Ray Van Neste who writes in his article, "The Lord's Supper in the Context of the Local Church," in the 2010 B&H publication, *The Lord's Supper: Remembering and Proclaiming Christ Until He Comes*:

In many Baptist churches, the deacons serve the elements . . . This is a fine practice, though we ought to be clear that the service in Acts 6 (keeping widows from starving) is significantly different from serving Communion. If the practice of deacons serving in this way helps to illustrate their role as servants, then this can be very fitting. However, we ought to be clear that others could also serve Communion. In my church, various men serve Communion.

→ **TEACHING TIP:** We must not assume that Baptist churches observe the Supper in the same way. Especially after Covid, many churches moved from passing Lord's Supper plates to using pre-packaged communion kits. In such cases, the deacons may still have a role in preparing for the supper.

- setting up the sanctuary for the observance of the Lord's Supper;

- distributing the elements of the Lord's Supper, if the elements are distributed in your congregation and not picked up by the congregation as they enter the sanctuary;

- cleaning up after the observance of the Lord's Supper;

- inviting the families of the church to both the observance of and a high view of the Lord's Supper;

- assisting the pastor in carrying the Lord's Supper to shut-ins or those who cannot come to the sanctuary.

IV. How Deacons Serve the Table of the Lord

We acknowledge the diversity of organizational structures within Baptist churches. The point of the The Three Tables model is not that a church with, say, a "Lord's Supper Committee" must disband that committee. Rather, this model is making a positive case for deacon involvement *in some capacity* in local churches for the reasons mentioned above. Deacons could quite easily and fruitfully work with other committees/teams and even with non-deacons who might serve the elements in given congregations to highlight our continuity with early Christian tradition and to highlight the servant-nature of deacons.

Think about your church and how it approaches The Table of the Lord. Is there a role for deacons at this table in your church? What does that role look like? What *might* it look like?→

→ **Teacher Tip:** Howard Foshee has written of one deacon's invaluable service at The Table of the Lord in his *Now That You're a Deacon*.

> An article in *The Deacon* told of an elderly deacon who has invested his time and talent in his church. A veteran Mississippi deacon, E.E. Tate, received a certificate from his church in recognition of "faithful service to the church, exercise of talents for the house of God, and giving without hope of recovery."

> The article stated: Believing that a new church should have new furniture, he started to work in his shop and made a communion table…

> He even made the church's communion trays. One pastor requested that Tate make a set of dual-purpose plates to allow serving of both the bread and the cup at the same time. This [set] is now used exclusively during the church's Lord's Supper services. Friends and associates readily admit that E.E. Tate is a deacon who has a great love for his church—a love that has grown through the years as he has advanced in age, matured in faith, and grown in grace.

> Thank God for deacons like E.E. Tate. There are legions like him who are happy stewards of their time and talents.

Session 4
The Second Table: The Table of the Poor (Part 1)

The church at Fenstanton, in 1652, adopted…several resolutions, on this subject…The following are the principal: "1. That it is the duty of persons that are in want, truly to declare their condition to the church or the deacons. 2. That after due examination had of the condition of any brother, by the deacon, they are to declare it to the congregation. 3. That if anyone belonging to the congregation hath any in want, that are nearly allied to him, he shall, to the utmost of his ability, relieve them, and not suffer them to be burdensome to the church. 4. That no person shall, at any time, be relieved by the congregation, but such as, to the utmost of his ability, does use all lawful means for his subsistence. 5. That if the congregation are not able to relieve those that are in want among them, but are obliged to send to other congregations, for help, they will not send any person in want, either with or without a letter, to gather their liberality for himself, but will send a man that is not in want, of whose fidelity they, have had experience, that he may receive their liberality, and bring it to the congregation.

Adam Taylor, *The History of the English General Baptists*

Acts 6

[1] Now in these days when the disciples were increasing in number, a complaint by the Hellenists arose against the Hebrews because their widows were being neglected in the daily distribution. [2] And the twelve summoned the full number of the disciples and said, "It is not right that we should give up preaching the word of God to serve tables. [3] Therefore, brothers, pick out from among you seven men of good repute, full of the Spirit and of wisdom, whom we will appoint to this duty. [4] But we will devote ourselves to prayer and to the ministry of the word."
[6] These they set before the apostles, and they prayed and laid their hands on them.
[7] And the word of God continued to increase, and the number of the disciples multiplied greatly in Jerusalem, and a great many of the priests became obedient to the faith.

I. The Historical Drift of Deacons from and Return of Deacons to "The Table of the Poor"

A summary of the evolution of deacon bodies:

1. 1st century — a **benevolence**/servant body

2. 1st-4th/5th centuries — a benevolence/servant body with **liturgical** responsibilities in corporate worship

(Fill in the Blanks:)

3. 15th century — almost exclusively liturgical/preparation for **priesthood**

4. 16th century — Reformation **return** to benevolence/service role[13]→

II. "The Table of the Poor" and Baptist Deacons

And what of Baptist Christians? Did early Baptists continue with the Reformation return of the office of deacon to serving "The Table of the Poor"?

In 1611, in the Baptist "Declaration of Faith of English People Remaining at Amsterdam in Holland," we read that "everie Church" should have "Elders" and "Deacons…who by their office releave the necessities off the poore and impotent brethre[n] concerning their bodies."[14] This confession then appeals to Acts 6:1–4 as biblical warrant for this view.

Article 19 of the 1660 London Baptist "Brief Confession or Declaration of Faith" reads:

That the poor saints belonging to the church of Christ are to be sufficiently provided for by the churches, that they neither want food or raiment, and this by a free and voluntary contribution (and not of necessity, or by the constraint or power of the magistrate), 2 Corinthians 9:7; 1 Corinthians 8:11,12, and this through the free and voluntary help of the deacons (called overseers of the poor), being faithful men, chosen by the church, and ordained by prayer and laying on of hands to that work. Acts 6:1, 2, 3, 4, 5, 6.

→ **Teaching Tip:** The German Protestant Reformer Martin Bucer made great efforts to stress care for the poor as a key ministry of deacons, as Jeannine Olson has aptly described in her 2005 history, *Deacons and Deaconesses Through the Centuries*:

Every church was to have deacons. All alms for the poor were to be directed through them. Deacons were to survey the poor carefully and assess their needs, visiting them and summoning them. There was to be no begging. Because the deacons were busy with the poor and with "discipline among the rest of the Christians," the care of the properties of the church and the collection of income belonged to "the office of subdeacons and administrators." However, deacons were to keep good records, both of the money at their disposal and of the poor, and to render their accounts to the bishop and presbytery.

The 1678 General Baptist "Orthodox Creed, or a Protestant Confession of Faith" referred to "deacons, or overseers of the poor."[15] In other words, they made the word "deacon" synonymous with "one who cares for the poor"!

The records of the Germantown, PA, Baptists reveal that their deacons oversaw the following purchases to help the poor:

- Jan. 12, 1752, To a poor woman whose child burnt itself: 7s. 6d.
- Nov. 18, 1752, To widows for meal (rye flour): 17s. 6d.
- Aug. 29, 1758, For the coffin of Sister Charitas: 17s.
- Dec. 7, 1762, To Sister Sophie for 1 cord of wood: £1, 8s.[16]→

III. The Modern Baptist Deacon and God's Heart for the Poor

What, then, are modern deacon bodies to do? In addition to understanding the strong historical emphasis on deacons as agents of serving the poor and needy in the early church, in the Reformation, and in Baptist history, each deacon must begin with recognizing the overwhelmingly powerful biblical emphasis on God's love for the poor.

1 Samuel 2

[8] He raises up the poor from the dust; he lifts the needy from the ash heap to make them sit with princes and inherit a seat of honor. For the pillars of the earth are the Lord's, and on them he has set the world.
Psalm 12

[5] "Because the poor are plundered, because the needy groan, I will now arise," says the Lord; "I will place him in the safety for which he longs."

Psalm 41

[1] Blessed is the one who considers the poor! In the day of trouble the Lord delivers him

---

→ **TEACHING TIP:** In his *History of the English General Baptists*, Adam Taylor writes that the General Baptists "were honourably distinguished" in their "maintenance of their poor." Taylor gives a very interesting look at the specifics of how these early Baptist deacons cared for those in need.

> The deacons, whose peculiar duty it was to superintend this part of the concerns of the church, were required to look out for proper objects and the poor were invited and encouraged to make their difficulties known to them. It was, indeed, esteemed disorderly to contract debts, before they had applied for relief to the church. It was the duty of the deacons to investigate the accuracy of the statements and, if necessary, to recommend them to the church.

Isaiah 25

[4] For you have been a stronghold to the poor, a stronghold to the needy in his distress, a shelter from the storm and a shade from the heat; for the breath of the ruthless is like a storm against a wall

Matthew 19

[21] Jesus said to him, "If you would be perfect, go, sell what you possess and give to the poor, and you will have treasure in heaven; and come, follow me."

Luke 4

[18] The Spirit of the Lord is upon me, because he has anointed me to proclaim good news to the poor. He has sent me to proclaim liberty to the captives and recovering of sight to the blind, to set at liberty those who are oppressed

Romans 15

[26] For Macedonia and Achaia have been pleased to make some contribution for the poor among the saints at Jerusalem.

2 Corinthians 8

[9] For you know the grace of our Lord Jesus Christ, that though he was rich, yet for your sake he became poor, so that you by his poverty might become rich.

Galatians 2

[10] Only, they asked us to remember the poor, the very thing I was eager to do.→

→ **TEACHING TIP:** Reading these accounts of the early Baptists and their efforts to serve "The Table of the Poor" might prove to be painful or awkward for some who are connected to deacon bodies that are not currently engaged in doing so. In some churches benevolence is that awkward elephant in the room that people do not quite know how to handle or else it is simply assumed that the paid staff should handle benevolence cases. Added to this, of course, is the fact that benevolence and handling it rightly requires time, can be complicated, and is not always easy. Regardless, caring for and tending to benevolence needs should be seen for what it is: a tremendous opportunity for deacons to demonstrate the very heart of God toward those in need or in distressing circumstances.

Session 5
"The Second Table: The Table of the Poor" (Part 2)

6. They are to take care of all Christ's poor, that they want nothing that is fitting for food and raiment, so far as the church is able to aid them.

7. They are to take care that neither covetousness or prodigality has any room in the church.

8. They are to visit the poor, and pray with them and for them when required.

9. They are to see to it that the rich have a liberal eye and a bountiful hand, and the poor a contented heart.

11. They must neither be harsh to the poor, nor flattering to the rich, but wholly impartial to all.

John Lacey, "The Duty and Office of Deacons," 18th century[17]

I. The Options before Us→

There would appear to be two viable options for deacons serving The Table of the Poor:

- Option 1: Deacons are only to minister to the poor of the **church**.

- Option 2: Deacons are to minister to the poor of the church and the poor **outside** the church though priority should be given to the former.

(Fill in the Blanks:)

→ **TEACHING TIP:** It is likely the case that the vast majority of deacons would agree that "the church" should care for the poor. Furthermore, they would likely agree that God cares deeply for the poor. Once these foundational premises are granted, however, a number of questions present themselves. For starters, to which "poor" are deacons to minister?

II. The Biblical Basis for Seeing the World at The Table of the Poor

- First, God's **heart** for the world.

John 3

[16] For God so loved the world . . .

- Second, God's **instructions** to Israel concerning outsiders.

Exodus 22

[21] You shall not wrong a sojourner or oppress him, for you were sojourners in the land of Egypt.

Leviticus 19

[10] And you shall not strip your vineyard bare, neither shall you gather the fallen grapes of your vineyard. You shall leave them for the poor and for the sojourner: I am the Lord your God.

- Third, the Romans' **amazement** at the early church's benevolence toward those outside the church.

Consider the words of the pagan Emperor Julian the Apostate to Arsacius, a pagan priest, in 362 AD concerning the Christians he had observed. He told Arsacius that "the impious Galilaeans [Christians] support not only their own poor but ours as well."[18] This as well as other evidence strongly suggests that the early church saw their mission as caring for all the poor, both the poor of the church and the poor of the world.

- Fourth, caring for the poor of the world does not mean the needs of the church should be **neglected**.

The 1765 Baptist "Records of a Church of Christ Meeting in Broadmead, Bristol":

> In this year it was resolved that the deacons should have power to relieve, out of the church's funds, poor persons of the Independent denomination, and also "other pious poor who were only hearers, and occasional poor who were here only in a transient way, who may be members of other churches, our own poor being first provided for."[19]

A rationale for this prioritizing of benevolence has been offered powerfully by J. Brown.

> Every poor and distressed man had a claim on me for pity, and, if I can afford it, for active exertion and pecuniary relief. But a poor Christian has a far stronger claim on my feelings, my labors, and my property. He is my brother, equally interested as myself in the blood and love of the Redeemer. I expect to spend an eternity with him in heaven. He is the representative of my unseen Savior, and he considers everything done to his poor afflicted as done to himself. For a Christian to be unkind to a Christian is not only wrong, it is monstrous.[20]

Perhaps it would be best to think of two *types* of benevolence instead of two *levels* of it.

- **Family** benevolence: meeting the needs of the church

- **Evangelistic** benevolence: meeting the needs of the hurting world in the name of Jesus→

→ **Teaching Tip:** It might be helpful for me to share how the church I pastor, Central Baptist Church in North Little Rock, Arkansas, handles benevolence. First, we have the following language in our By-laws:

> The deacon body of Central Baptist Church is hereby given the following critical functions:
>
> 1. First and foremost, they are tasked with handling the benevolence ministry of Central Baptist Church. They shall work with the pastoral staff in developing programs to assist members of Central Baptist Church with special needs including but not limited to assisting widows, shut-ins, and the poor within our church body.
>
> 2. Second, they will work to meet the physical needs of the needy in our community in a way that will open the door for the deacons to share the gospel and the love of Christ.

You will notice the two types of benevolence: family benevolence and evangelistic benevolence. You will also notice that the deacons, while tasked with "handling" benevolence, are to work with the pastoral staff in thinking through the best way of doing this.

What this looks like at Central Baptist Church is a series of three rotating teams within our deacon body that correspond to the three tables being discussed in this study: The Table of the Lord, The Table of the Poor, and The Table of the Pastor. Our deacon body is divided by three with each group serving a table. Every four months the tables rotate. Thus, every year every deacon will serve on each table. (*continued*)

When a benevolence request comes into Central Baptist Church, either through a church member or somebody walking in off the street, our staff assesses the situation and whether or not it is a small enough matter that the staff can meet directly out of benevolence petty cash kept in the office or whether it needs to be referred to our deacons. When a request for help needs to be referred, a member of the benevolence team is contacted and the relevant information is given to them. A member of the team looks into the request and talks to the person making it. If it is under a certain monetary limit and the benevolence team is in agreement that it should be met, they make arrangements to meet the need. If it is over a certain limit, it requires a vote of the entire deacon body. If, for whatever reason, there are reservations about the request, the request for help could be denied. We work very hard to try to lean toward grace and not to be unduly skeptical, yet good stewardship demands that we make sure that we can meet the need in good conscience.

The deacon benevolence fund is built up each month at our Lord's Supper observances. After each observance, the deacons stand at the door with a plate to receive a benevolence offering. One hundred percent of that offering goes to help those in need. The deacons collect and administer those funds.

We do not claim that this is a perfect model, but we do claim that it is viable and that it can be a helpful tool in leading deacons to serve "The Table of the Poor."

Session 6
"The Third Table: The Table of the Pastor" (Part 1)

H.I. Hester, faithful pastor, teacher, and denominational leader, once told me of an incident that occurred in the 1930's while he was serving a church in Missouri. "One night a gang robbed our local bank. When the night watchman, who was a member of our church, appeared, he was shot down. He was rushed to the hospital but died four days later. This naturally created a sensation so that there was an overflow crowd at the funeral service. In this funeral service I spoke out strongly against such criminal acts. At the time the criminals had not been apprehended. Several years later I learned that three deacons at the service, fearing that some member of the gang might attack me on my way home, quietly followed my car the entire ten miles back to my home in Liberty, Missouri. This deed of courage and loyalty has meant much to me through the years."

Howard B. Foshee, *Now That You're a Deacon*[21]

I. On the Unity of the Pastor and the Deacons

Among the many charming treasures one can find in the historical records of the wonderful and sometimes odd people called "Baptists" is the following entry in George Yuille's *History of the Baptists in Scotland* about Crown Terrace Church.

> The history of the Church can be traced back to the year 1820…Mr. John Inkster was the first Pastor, and a native of Burra Isle…A unique thing in connection with his long and faithful ministry is the fact that the two Deacons who assisted him were both called John Inkster, and that these three John Inksters, one of whom was the presentor, sat at the Lord's Table every Lord's Day for forty years, till one of the three was "called home," leaving the Pastor and the other John Inkster to work together as true yoke-fellows for a period, in all, of 52 years.[22]

The Inkster Challenge:

A pastor and his deacons should be so united that they could, in essence, have the same **name**. Our bond should be such that to see the pastor is to see the deacons and to see the deacons is to see the pastor. May we all be John Inksters!

Consider the harmonious imagery of Philippians 1 when Paul sends his greetings to the church.

[1] Paul and Timothy, servants of Christ Jesus, to all the saints in Christ Jesus who are at Philippi, *with the overseers and deacons*

That "with" is significant. The "overseers" and "deacons" are pictured by Paul as together and united as one in caring for the body of Christ!

On the other end of the spectrum we might think of the following story of deacon-pastor *disharmony* from Paul Powell.

. . . One of my preacher boys called me one day and said he was having trouble with four of his deacons. These four deacons had run off the last four pastors in the church and now they were giving him trouble. He said, "What should I do? Should I square off and fight them? Should I take a baseball bat to them? How should I handle it?

I told him to be very patient, gentle, and kind. Time takes care of a lot of things.

Sure enough, the next time I saw him he told me how things had worked out. He said one of those deacons was working in his yard one Saturday when he suddenly was struck with a heart attack and died. He said he would preach the funeral and the other three men served as pall-bearers. Then, a few weeks later, a second of those deacons was driving to work when he was hit by an eighteen-wheeler and killed instantly. He said that he preached the funeral and the other two served as pall-bearers.

Then, he said, the third of those men learned that he had cancer, it had spread rapidly, and within a few weeks he was dead. He said that he preached the funeral and the one remaining man assisted as a pall bearer.

Following the last funeral the remaining deacon rode with him back to the church. In their conversation he leaned over and said, "Preacher, I want you to know I have been on your side all the time."[23]

Of what does the relationship between the pastor and the deacon consist? Put another way, how do deacons serve "The Table of the Pastor"?

II. The Service of Understanding

Howard Foshee recommended the following for deacons:

1. **Understand** your pastor and his work.

2. **Pray** with and for your pastor.

3. **Affirm** your pastor.

4. **Support** your pastor.

5. **Enjoy** fellowship with your pastor.[24]

III. The Service of Freedom

Deacons are to free their pastors to do the work to which they were called. Consider:

Acts 6

[1] Now in these days when the disciples were increasing in number, a complaint by the Hellenists arose against the Hebrews because their widows were being neglected in the daily distribution. [2] And the twelve summoned the full number of the disciples and said, "It is not right that we should give up preaching the word of God to serve tables. [3] Therefore, brothers, pick out from among you seven men of good repute, full of the Spirit and of wisdom, whom we will appoint to this duty. [4] *But we will devote ourselves to prayer and to the ministry of the word."*

This is not to say that pastors will only be able to focus all of their time on "preaching the word," "prayer," and "the ministry of the word."

It is to say, however, that if the demands of pastoral ministry in a local church are such that a pastor is not able to pray, study the word, and prepare adequately for the proclamation of the word, then something is **wrong**.→

IV. The Service of Assistance

The greatest way that deacons can assist their pastors is by being engaged with the **families** of the church entrusted to their care in such a way that meaningful relationships can be formed between the deacons and the members.→

Elton Trueblood suggests that, in some ways, deacons may be able to minister to members of the church more effectively than pastors.

> First, the layman does not have to bear the stigma of being a clergyman. The clergyman is often expected to be a 'good' person. He is supposed to visit the sick, to care for people. After all, 'this is what he is paid to do.' Whereas, the layman is free from any of these expectations and, thus, his presence is often taken more seriously. Second, the layman is often closer to common life. He is already in the factory, the bank, the office, the school, and, thus, does not have to gain entrance from the outside. Third, the lay minister has a certain freshness. Often the training of the clergymen blinds him to possible new ways of doing and thinking, whereas the layman can bring a freshness to the task.[25]

Do you agree with Trueblood's assessment? Why or Why not?

→ **Teaching Tip:** This is where deacons come in. They watch and ask their pastors, "Are we helping to free you to be able to bring to us the Word of God? Are you able to pray and plead to God on behalf of this church?" If the pastor answers "No" and if this answer is a result of unrealistic ministry demands and not his own laziness and bad priorities, then the deacons must step in, evaluate, and help relieve the burden. In any given context there will be more than enough for deacons to do to help free their pastors.

→ **Teaching Tip:** In our church the tool by which we have chosen to organize this is the "Authentic Family Ministry Plan" (which we previously referred to by its more well-known name, "Deacon Family Ministry"), a plan which divides the membership of the church up among the deacons who then minister to their allotted families. At Central Baptist, members voluntarily "opt in" to the "Authentic Family Ministry," with the exception of our very elderly members and shut-ins who are simply added. I can say from personal experience that the single most important service the deacons can offer the church is the service of caring for, being there for, checking on, and ministering to the families of the church. *Virtually every pastor I know would say that deacons helping them minister to the members of the church so that the full brunt of the great needs present in any congregation does not fall solely on their shoulders would be the single greatest thing deacons could do to help them.*

Interestingly, both the deacon service of freedom and the service of assistance find an Old Testament foundation in Jethro's advice to his son-in-law Moses, recorded in Exodus 18.

[13] The next day Moses sat to judge the people, and the people stood around Moses from morning till evening. [14] When Moses' father-in-law saw all that he was doing for the people, he said, "What is this that you are doing for the people? Why do you sit alone, and all the people stand around you from morning till evening?" [15] And Moses said to his father-in-law, "Because the people come to me to inquire of God; [16] when they have a dispute, they come to me and I decide between one person and another, and I make them know the statutes of God and his laws." [17] Moses' father-in-law said to him, "What you are doing is not good. [18] You and the people with you will certainly wear yourselves out, for the thing is too heavy for you. You are not able to do it alone. [19] Now obey my voice; I will give you advice, and God be with you! You shall represent the people before God and bring their cases to God, [20] and you shall warn them about the statutes and the laws, and make them know the way in which they must walk and what they must do. [21] Moreover, look for able men from all the people, men who fear God, who are trustworthy and hate a bribe, and place such men over the people as chiefs of thousands, of hundreds, of fifties, and of tens. [22] And let them judge the people at all times. Every great matter they shall bring to you, but any small matter they shall decide themselves. So it will be easier for you, and they will bear the burden with you. [23] If you do this, God will direct you, you will be able to endure, and all this people also will go to their place in peace."

In what ways did Jethro's advice provide the service of freedom? How did it free Moses to do what God had called him to do?

By appointing others to handle the commonplace disputes of the people, all of that time would now be freed up for Moses to focus on the greater tasks before him and to be the leader that the people needed.

In what ways did Jethro's advice provide the service of assistance? How did it lead to the families and individuals of Israel being more effectively cared for?

It provided the service of assistance in that by appointing overseers for smaller groups the people of Israel would have received more careful attention from clearer and less-exhausted minds that could give them their full attention.

Session 7
"The Third Table: The Table of the Pastor" (Part 2)

The relation of deacons to the pastor will necessarily be a close one. These are the two divinely appointed offices in the New Testament church and were set up for the watch-care of the membership. The church will only progress in the work of the Lord as these two offices harmonize their efforts. The board of deacons was never intended to lord it over the pastor. Neither is the pastor a dictator over the board of deacons. The pastor is the elected leader of the church. The office of deacon has been created to give assistance to the pastor. There is an interrelation between the two offices. The pastor does not order the deacons. The pastor accepts them as co-workers in the area of pastoral leadership. As he confides in the deacons and relies upon them for service, they recognize his leadership and follow his counsel in the work of the church.

J.D. O'Donnell, Handbook for Deacons[26]

I. The Service of Support

Deacons can also serve "The Table of the Pastor" by **supporting** him and, when needed, **defending** him.→

Pastors are not above criticism or critique, but, as a general rule, if a deacon has a complaint that is significant enough to be said **about** his pastor he has a complaint that is significant enough to say **to** his pastor.

→ **TEACHING TIP:** An example of the *opposite* of support would be the following statement found in a 1795 Baptist circular letter by an Elder Powers:

> A preacher was once ordained in North Wales—after the rites were performed, one of the deacons took him by the hand and saluted him thus: "God bless you, my Brother, and keep you humble, for we intend to keep you poor."

(Drawing given to Wyman Richardson by some of his deacons at
First Baptist Church, Dawson, Georgia, circa 2009)

II. The Service of Peacemaking

A final way that deacons can serve "The Table of the Pastor" is
through the service of **peacemaking**.

Matthew 5

9 Blessed are the peacemakers, for they shall be called sons of God.

Mark 5

34 And he said to her, "Daughter, your faith has made you well; go in peace, and be healed of your disease."

Mark 9

50 Salt is good, but if the salt has lost its saltiness, how will you make it salty again? Have salt in yourselves, and be at peace with one another."

Luke 2

14 "Glory to God in the highest, and on earth peace among those with whom he is pleased!"

Luke 24

36 As they were talking about these things, Jesus himself stood among them, and said to them, "Peace to you!"

John 14

27 Peace I leave with you; my peace I give to you. Not as the world gives do I give to you. Let not your hearts be troubled, neither let them be afraid.

John 16

33 I have said these things to you, that in me you may have peace. In the world you will have tribulation. But take heart; I have overcome the world."

Fill in
the Blanks:

In any given church, the deacons must be **agents** of peace, they must offer the service of peacemaking!

"The first deacons served as peacemakers," writes Ken Howerton.[27] He is correct. Let us turn again to Acts 6.

[1] Now in these days when the disciples were increasing in number, a complaint by the Hellenists arose against the Hebrews because their widows were being neglected in the daily distribution. [2] And the twelve summoned the full number of the disciples and said, "It is not right that we should give up preaching the word of God to serve tables. [3] Therefore, brothers, pick out from among you seven men of good repute, full of the Spirit and of wisdom, whom we will appoint to this duty. [4] But we will devote ourselves to prayer and to the ministry of the word." [5] And what they said pleased the whole gathering, and they chose Stephen, a man full of faith and of the Holy Spirit, and Philip, and Prochorus, and Nicanor, and Timon, and Parmenas, and Nicolaus, a proselyte of Antioch. [6] These they set before the apostles, and they prayed and laid their hands on them. [7] And the word of God continued to increase, and the number of the disciples multiplied greatly in Jerusalem, and a great many of the priests became obedient to the faith.

Notice the progression:

Fill in the Blanks:

- There was **conflict** in the church and a portion of the church had "a complaint."

- **Deacons** were chosen.

- The conflict was **resolved** and peace and growth returned to the church.

Deacons: *peacemaking is in the very DNA of the deacon body!* It is part of your original charter. The deacon's job is to maintain, guard, and keep peace. J.D. O'Donnell has spoken well to this:

In his position as a leader in the church, the deacon can promote the harmony of the church. The seven chosen men in Acts 6 healed a breach in the church fellowship and restored harmony to the church. Factions are often promoted by deacons rather than healed by them. No deacon should ever be guilty of this. As a layman he can often feel the pulse of the people in ways that the pastor cannot. When he is aware of dissension or any dissatisfaction among the members, the deacon should labor to resolve the problem. If there is any murmuring against the pastor, he should work to maintain the respect of the members for the pastor's leadership. He has no right to promote disharmony in the church.[28]

Appendix 1
The Three Tables: A Planning Worksheet for Deacon Bodies

List below the appropriate heading how the deacon
body might serve that particular table in your church.
(See Appendix 2 on page 35 for an example of what this might look like.)

The Table of the Lord

The Table of the Poor

The Table of the Pastor

Appendix 2
The Three Tables at Central Baptist Church, North Little Rock, AR

The Table of the Lord

- deacons set up the sanctuary for the Lord's Supper each month

- deacons clean up after Lord's Supper services

- deacons keep an eye on the Lord's Supper supply level

The Table of the Poor

- deacons handle major benevolence requests

- deacons collect monthly benevolence offerings at the back door of the church after our monthly Lord's Supper

- deacons conduct a deacon food drive for our food pantry each Christmas season

- deacons are available to assist in counseling re:benevolence situations

The Table of the Pastor

- deacons contact their "Authentic Family Ministry" families monthly

- deacons pray for families and for the pastor and staff

- deacons advise pastor on difficult situations when approached for wisdom

- deacons help with special services: assisting on Maundy Thursday, Good Friday, and Christmas Eve

Endnotes

1. James B. Taylor, *Virginia Baptist Ministers First Series*, 343. Most of the quotations from Baptist primary sources used in this workbook are from the Baptist Standard Bearer's 2005 Baptist Heritage Series collection.

2. J. B. Link, *Texas Historical and Biographical Magazine*, vol. 2, 458.

3. Ken Howerton, *Pastor and Deacons: Servants Working Together*. (Emerald House Group, Inc., 2019), Kindle Location 1485.

4. Patricia Marks, "Holy and Unholy Deacons in Late Nineteenth-Century Popular Verse." *Christianity and Literature* 61:2 (Winter 2012) 241–55.

5. J. H. Spencer, *A History of Kentucky Baptists*. Vol. 2. 386.

6. Robert Baylor Semple, *History of the Baptists in Virginia*, 133.

7. Matt Smethurst, *Deacons: How They Serve and Strengthen the Church*. Wheaton, IL: Crossway, 2021.

8. Jesse Mercer, *History of the Georgia Baptist Association*, 114–17.

9. James Leo Garrett Jr., "Professor Examines Historical Role of Deacons (Part 2)." *Baptist Standard* (June 26, 1991) 12.

10. David Spencer, *The Early Baptists of Philadelphia*, 69.

11. Nathan E. Wood, *The History of the First Baptist Church of Boston*, 158.

12. W. J. McGlothlin, *Baptist Confessions of Faith*, 243.

13. Jeannine Olson, *Deacons and Deaconesses Through the Centuries*. (St. Louis, MO: Concordia Publishing House, 2005), Kindle Locations 1988–2001.

14. W. J. McGlothlin, *Baptist Confessions of Faith*, 65.

15. Edward Bean Underhill, *Confessions of Faith and Other Public Documents*, 86, 108.

16. Martin Grove Brumbaugh, *A History of The German Baptist Brethren in Europe and America*, 1899.

17. Joseph Ivimey, *A History of the English Baptists*, Vol. 4., 370.

18. Peter Brown, *Poverty and Leadership in the Later Roman Empire*, 2.

19. Edward Terrill, "The Records of A Church of Christ Meeting in Broadmead, Bristol," 237.

20. Quoted in Timothy George, *Galatians*. (Nashville, TN: Broadman and Holman, 1994), 425.

21. Howard B. Foshee, *Now That You're a Deacon*. (Nashville, TN: B&H Books, 1975), 37–38.

22. George Yuille, *History of the Baptists in Scotland*, 93–94.

23. Paul Powell, *The Church*. (Dallas, TX: The Annuity Board of the Southern Baptist Convention, 1997), 173.

24. Foshee, *Now That You're a Deacon*, 38.

25. Quoted in Foshee, *Now That You're a Deacon*, 19.

26. J.D. O'Donnell, *Handbook for Deacons*. (Nashville, TN: Randall House Publications, 1973), 53.

27. Howerton, *Pastor and Deacons: Servants Working Together*, Kindle Location 1428.

28. O'Donnell, *Handbook for Deacons*, 17.